Solomon the Superintendent

Elizabeth Neblett

PEARSON
Longman

Modern Dramas 1: Solomon the Superintendent
First Edition

Copyright © 2008

Pearson Education, Inc.
10 Bank Street, White Plains, NY 10606

Staff credits: The people who made up the *Modern Dramas 1: Solomon the Superintendent* team, representing editorial, production, design, and manufacturing, include Ann France, Laura Le Dréan, Martha McGaughey, Jaime Lieber, and Michael Mone.

Cover design: Ann France
Cover illustration: Lyle Miller
Text design: Ann France
Text composition: S4Carlisle Publishing Services
Text font: 12.5/13 Minion
Illustrations: Lyle Miller

ISBN-13: 978-0-13-235531-5
ISBN-10:   0-13-235531-0

LONGMAN ON THE **WEB**

Pearsonlongman.com offers online resources for teachers and students. Access our Companion Websites, our online catalog, and our local offices around the world.

Visit us at **www.pearsonlongman.com**.

Printed in the United States of America
1 2 3 4 5 6 7 8 9 10—DJC—12 11 10 09 08 07

Contents

To the Teacher

Solomon the Superintendent is the first book in the series of four Longman *Modern Dramas*. These dramas provide authentic, level-appropriate, engaging literature for adult English language learners. The individual episodes of the books can either stand alone or be taught in sequence as part of an ongoing course. *Modern Dramas* fill the need in the beginning to low-intermediate classroom for controlled reading material of more than a few paragraphs. *Modern Dramas* also keep the students interested in what they are reading: They will want to keep turning the pages to find out what happens next.

You will be amazed at how engaged your students will be with these stories. The involving story lines will draw students in, and motivate them to keep on reading. The language is not completely grammatically controlled; *Modern Dramas* aim above all to be interesting and natural, and have been written with an eye to research that shows that most students' reading ability is at a higher level than their speaking, listening, or writing skills. By the last episode, your students will be able to follow the plot and to answer the reading comprehension questions without using their dictionaries.

In this first book of the series, nine episodes follow the story of Solomon the Superintendent as he copes with the challenges of his life and his job. Students learn vocabulary related to job skills, employment, and life in an apartment building.

Each of the nine episodes consists of:

- **The opening page**
  A picture sparks student interest in the episode to come, and provides a springboard for lively student discussion.

- **Get Ready to Read**
  The two questions about the opening art can be discussed in pairs, small groups, or with the whole class. These questions focus students' attention on the theme of the episode. An exercise after these questions introduces new vocabulary. The form of this exercise varies so as to keep students engaged: multiple choice, matching definitions, matching pictures, and matching words to their opposites.

- **In the last episode . . .**
  Each episode starts with a brief summary of the previous episode, so that students who were absent will be able to follow the story, and students who have been in class will be reminded of what has already happened.

- **The reading**
  Each reading is between 600 and 1,000 words. You can assign the episode and the exercises following it for homework, but it is also useful to read it aloud to the class, or to have the students listen to the recording of the episode before they read it on their own. New vocabulary not targeted on the opening page is defined either with small illustrations or with a gloss on the relevant page.

- **Reading Comprehension**
  These true/false and multiple-choice questions check students' understanding of what they have just read. The exercises can be used for class discussion. You can encourage students to explain their answers or tell the class where in the episode they found the information to answer the questions.

- **Work with the Words**
  These exercises review and solidify students' knowledge of new vocabulary, both the words targeted on the opening page and other vocabulary words which have come up in the reading. The exercises are multiple choice, fill in the blank, and select the opposite word, among others.

- **Lifeskill Practice**
  These exercises focus on a particular theme or competency featured in the episode. The exercises reinforce standard life skills and competencies.

- **Dialogue Practice**
  Selected portions of the episode are reproduced at the end of each of the nine segments so that students can practice the language in a focused way. These can be used for pronunciation practice or role play.

After your students finish *Solomon the Superintendent*, they will be eager to read the other books in the *Modern Dramas* series: *Lucy and the Piano Player*, *Victor's Secret*, and *Ramona Goes Back to Mexico*.

Meet Solomon

Get Ready to Read

A Discuss with a partner.

1. Do you live in an apartment or in a house?
2. Do you have a **super**[*] in your building?

B Match the words with the definitions.

  d   **1.** meals   **a.** often; most of the time

_____ **2.** usually   **b.** not sick; in good physical condition

_____ **3.** tenant   **c.** not with other people

_____ **4.** elderly   **d.** breakfast, lunch, dinner

_____ **5.** alone   **e.** person who rents a house or apartment

_____ **6.** in good health   **f.** old

---

[*]**super** or **superintendent** = a person who fixes problems in an apartment building

It's seven o'clock in the evening. Solomon Soriano and his family are getting ready for dinner. Solomon is the **super** for the apartment building at 112 Standish Avenue, and he's **usually** very busy. He doesn't have much time to eat **meals** with his family, but tonight it's quiet. His wife, Virginia, and his three children, Samuel, 9, Steven, 10, and Susana, 16, are having dinner together for the first time this month. Susana is putting the dishes on the table, Samuel is **pouring** the water, and Steven is putting a bowl of salad on the table. Solomon is putting spaghetti in a large bowl, and Virginia is taking the garlic bread out of the oven. Everything is ready. Then, *ring, ring!* The telephone is ringing!

pour

"Oh, no," says Solomon. "Maybe it's a wrong number."

"Don't answer it, Daddy," says Susana.

"I'm the super," says Solomon. "I have to answer the phone."

He answers the phone.

"Hello?"

"Hello, Mr. Soriano? This is Mrs. Clark, in 4E."

"Hello, Mrs. Clark. How are you this evening?"

Mrs. Clark is one of the **tenants** in the building. She's **elderly**, 78 years old, and she lives **alone**. Her children are married and live in a different city, but Mrs. Clark is **in good health**, and she loves to talk.

"I'm fine, Mr. Soriano, but I have a problem in my apartment. Can you come up right away?"

"What's the problem, Mrs. Clark?"

"Oh, it will only take a minute. Please, can you come right now?"

"All right, Mrs. Clark. I'll be right there."

Virginia asks, "Mrs. Clark again? She always calls at dinnertime. What does she want now?"

"Now, honey, be nice. Mrs. Clark is an elderly woman. She's 78. She needs help. I'll be right back."

tool kit

Solomon gets his **tool kit** and goes to the stairs. He walks up to the fourth floor and **knocks** on the door of Apartment 4E.

"Who is it?"

"It's Solomon Soriano, Mrs. Clark."

knock

Mrs. Clark opens the door very slowly. First she opens one **lock**, then a second lock, and finally, she opens the third lock.

"Thank you for coming, Mr. Soriano."

"What's the problem, Mrs. Clark?" Solomon looks around. He doesn't see any problems.

"It's in the kitchen. Come with me."

Solomon goes with Mrs. Clark into the kitchen.

lock

"Do you see that bag of sugar on the third shelf of the **cabinet**?" Mrs. Clark is pointing to the third shelf.

"Yes, I do." Solomon looks up at the cabinet.

"Can you get that bag? I can't get it."

Solomon gets the bag of sugar. He gives it to Mrs. Clark.

"Oh, thank you, Mr. Soriano. Now I can make my dessert. I didn't have any sugar."

cabinet

"Was that the problem, Mrs. Clark?"

"Well, yes. I can't make my special cake without sugar, can I?"

"No, you can't. Well, I'm going back to my dinner. See you later, Mrs. Clark."

Solomon goes back to his apartment. He gets his dinner out of the oven.
"Now, we can eat together as a family."
Solomon is eating his spaghetti. "Virginia, this is great garlic bread. Did you make it?"
"No, I didn't," says Virginia. "Susana made it."
"Susana, this is delicious. It's . . ."
Ring! Ring! The phone is ringing again.

Reading Comprehension

A Circle *True* or *False*.

1. Solomon lives in a house.	True	False
2. Solomon is married.	True	False
3. Solomon has three sons.	True	False
4. Solomon always has dinner with his family.	True	False
5. Solomon's family is eating cake.	True	False
6. Solomon has to answer the phone.	True	False
7. Mrs. Clark lives alone.	True	False

B Circle the correct answer.

1. Solomon's wife's name is _____.
   a. Virginia   **b.** Susana   **c.** Mrs. Clark

2. Where does Solomon live?
   a. in a house   **b.** in Standish   **c.** on Standish Avenue

3. Mrs. Clark lives _____.
   a. with her husband   **b.** with her children   **c.** alone

Who said it? Write the sentences under the correct person's name.

Can you come up right away?	I have to answer the phone.
I didn't have any sugar.	Now I can make my dessert.
I'll be right back.	Now we can eat together as a family.

Mrs. Clark	Solomon

Work with the Words

  Circle the correct answer.

1. Solomon is **usually** very busy. What does **usually** mean?
   a. Solomon is busy many days each week.
   b. Solomon is busy every weekend.
   c. Solomon is busy one day a week.

2. Which one is a **meal**?
   a. lunch   b. dish   c. bacon

3. What do you **pour**?

    a. water   **b.** garlic bread   **c.** cookies

4. Who is not **in good health**?

    a.   **b.**   **c.**

5. A **tenant** _____ a building.

    a. lives in   **b.** fixes problems in   **c.** paints

6. Mrs. Clark is **elderly**. She is _____.

    a. young   **b.** old   **c.** beautiful

7. What does a **super** do?

    a. sells apartments   **b.** buys apartments   **c.** fixes problems in apartments

B   Complete the sentences with the correct words.

cabinet	knocks	locks	pours	tool kit

1. Mrs. Clark's sugar is in the _____.

2. Solomon takes his _____ to Mrs. Clark's apartment.

3. Samuel _____ water into his glass.

4. Mrs. Clark has three _____ on her door.

5. Solomon _____ on Mrs. Clark's door.

Lifeskill Practice

■ Use *do* to ask about jobs.

Circle the answers.

1. **Q:** What does a super do?
   A: A super _____.

   fixes problems in a building

   fixes computer problems

   answers the phone

   lives and works in the building

   cooks dinner

   makes a cake

2. **Q:** What does a cook do?
   A: A cook _____.

   makes a cake

   makes breakfast

   makes beds

   lives in a restaurant

   works in a restaurant

   fixes computer problems

Dialogue Practice

Practice the conversation with two classmates.

Solomon: Oh, no! Maybe it's a wrong number.

Susana: Don't answer it, Daddy.

Solomon: I'm the super. I have to answer the phone. Hello?

Mrs. Clark: Hello, Mr. Soriano? This is Mrs. Clark, in 4E.

Solomon: Hello, Mrs. Clark. How are you this evening?

Mrs. Clark: I'm fine, Mr. Soriano, but I have a problem in my apartment. Can you come up right away?

Solomon: What's the problem, Mrs. Clark?

Mrs. Clark: Oh, it will only take a minute. Please, can you come right now?

Solomon: All right, Mrs. Clark. I'll be right there.

You Need an Assistant!

Get Ready to Read

Discuss with a partner.

1. What kind of problems do you have in your home?
2. How long do you wait to fix a problem in your house or apartment—one day, two days, one week?

B Circle the correct definition.

1. **appointment**
   a. a bill you have to pay
   b. a date to see someone at a particular time

2. **during**
   a. at the same time
   b. at a different time

3. A **receptionist** _____.
   a. answers the phone and takes messages
   b. cooks dinner

4. *I will* **hire** *you* means _____.
   a. I will not give you a job
   b. I will give you a job

5. *He* (or *She*) *is* **cute** means _____.
   a. pretty (female or baby) or handsome (male)
   b. polite

6. My **assistant** is _____.
   a. my helper
   b. my boss

🎧 *In the last episode ...*

Solomon Soriano is the superintendent at 112 Standish Avenue. He's very busy, so he can't spend a lot of time with his wife, Virginia, and their three children, Susana, Samuel, and Steven. He can't always eat dinner with them because the telephone rings at dinnertime.

It's eight-thirty in the evening, and Solomon is at home in his apartment. Mrs. Clark, an elderly tenant in the building, called him three times **during** dinner. Now his dinner is cold, and Virginia, Solomon's wife, is **angry**. Solomon is putting his spaghetti dinner in the microwave.

angry

"Solomon," she says, "you have to speak to Mrs. Clark! She called three times during dinner. We **never*** have time to eat as a family. We never go out because your cell phone rings and you have to come back to the building. We never take a vacation. We never . . ."

"I know, I know. But I feel sorry for Mrs. Clark. She lives alone, and her children live far away. I think she calls me because she wants someone to talk to."

"But your children want to talk to you, too, Solomon. Steven and Samuel have a baseball game tomorrow night, and they want you to come to their game," says Virginia. "I have an idea! Maybe you can get an **assistant**!"

assistant

"An assistant?" asks Solomon. "That's a good idea. I have a lot of work, and I'm very busy. I'll call my boss, Mr. Morgan. If he says it's OK, I'll have more free time. Maybe I can eat dinner with the family every night, and maybe we can take a vacation!"

Two days later, Solomon goes downtown to see his boss, Mr. Morgan. Mr. Morgan has ten apartment buildings and

***never** = the opposite of *always*

works in a large office building. Solomon talks to Linda, the **receptionist**.

"Good morning. May I help you?" Linda asks.

"Yes, please. I have an **appointment** with Mr. Morgan. My name is Solomon Soriano."

receptionist

"Have a seat, Mr. Soriano. Mr. Morgan is on the phone. I'll tell him that you're here."

Five minutes later, Linda says, "Mr. Soriano, Mr. Morgan is ready for you." Mr. Morgan shakes Solomon's hand. "Good morning, Solomon. Is everything OK at 112 Standish?"

"Yes, sir, but I have a problem," says Solomon. Solomon is always **nervous** when he talks to Mr. Morgan. "I'm very busy. I go from apartment to apartment to fix problems. There are always phone calls at my meal time, and I don't see my family. I think I need some help with the building."

appointment

Mr. Morgan **agrees**.* "Yes, Solomon," he says, "you're right. You need some help. 112 Standish has 24 apartments, and it's an old building. It needs a lot of repairs. You can hire a part-time assistant. We'll put an **ad**** in the paper this weekend."

On Saturday, there is an **advertisement**** in the newspaper.

nervous

Saturday evening and all day Sunday, Solomon's phone rings, but some people have no experience.

"Hello?"

"Hello, I'm calling about the ad."

"Hello. I'm the super, and I'm looking for an assistant. Tell me about your experience."

"Oh, I have a lot of experience. I can fix any car."

"Any car? But I'm a super. Can you fix a kitchen sink?"

"A kitchen sink? No, but I can fix a Toyota."

agree

*agree = say *yes* to someone

**ad or advertisement = a short message in a newspaper; announces a job or something for sale

"Thank you for calling, but I need someone with building experience."

Many people call. Finally, on Sunday night, Solomon **hires** a new assistant, a young man named Bob Crespo. He's about 21 years old. Bob has a good reference from his high school teacher, and he is very friendly. Susana, Solomon's daughter, thinks Bob is **cute**. "Call me Bobby," he says.

Solomon asks Bobby, "Can you start tomorrow?"

Bobby answers, "Sure, Mr. Soriano. What time tomorrow?"

Solomon thinks for a moment. "Come at eight o'clock."

"OK, Mr. Soriano," says Bobby, "I'll see you at eight o'clock sharp. Nice to meet you, Mr. Soriano, and it was nice to meet you, too, Susana." Then he leaves.

"See you tomorrow, Bobby," says Susana.

Reading Comprehension

A Circle *True* or *False*.

1. Mrs. Clark called four times.	True	False
2. Solomon's dinner is cold.	True	False
3. Virginia is happy about Mrs. Clark.	True	False
4. Linda works for Mr. Morgan.	True	False
5. Solomon's family takes a vacation every year.	True	False
6. Bobby is friendly.	True	False
7. Solomon's sons play football.	True	False

B Circle the correct answer.

1. Solomon needs _____.
   a. a new wife   **b.** a new job   **c.** an assistant

2. Solomon thinks an assistant is _____.
   a. a good idea   **b.** a bad idea   **c.** expensive

3. Solomon needs an assistant to help him with _____.
   a. his children   **b.** the building   **c.** his car

C Put the following sentences in order from 1 to 6.

____ Virginia is angry and tells Solomon to ask for an assistant.

____ Solomon talks to the receptionist.

____ Mr. Morgan puts an ad in the newspaper.

_1_ Mrs. Clark calls Solomon many times.

____ Solomon hires Bobby Crespo.

____ Solomon misses dinner with his family.

Work with the Words

A Circle the correct answer.

1. Virginia is **angry**.

a.    b. 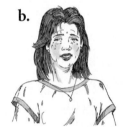   c.

2. Solomon is **nervous** when he goes to talk to his boss.

a.    b    c.

3. I use my cell phone during _____.
   a. lunch
   b. my English class
   c. an appointment with my boss

4. Mrs. Clark lives **alone**. Who lives with her?

   a. her children   **b.** a dog   **c.** no one

5. Solomon thinks an assistant is a good idea. He **agrees** with his wife. Solomon and his wife have _____.

   a. the same opinion

   b. a different opinion

   c. no opinion

B Complete the sentences with the correct words.

ad	agrees	alone	hires	never

1. Bobby has good references, so Solomon _____ him.

2. Bobby read the _____ in the newspaper and called Solomon about the job.

3. Solomon doesn't live _____; he lives with his wife and children.

4. Mr. Morgan _____ with Solomon; Solomon needs an assistant.

5. Virginia says that the family _____ takes a vacation.

Lifeskill Practice

■ Here's a conversation before an appointment.

A Put the sentences from a conversation in the correct order.

_____ Thank you. I can wait a few minutes.

_1_ May I help you?

_____ Ms. Jones is on the phone now. Have a seat.

_____ Ms. Jones can see you now.

_____ Hi. I have an appointment with Ms. Jones.

B Practice the conversation with a classmate.

Dialogue Practice

Practice the conversation with a classmate.

Solomon: Hello?

Caller: Hello. I'm calling about the ad.

Solomon: Hello. I'm the super, and I'm looking for an assistant. Tell me about your experience.

Caller: Oh, I have a lot of experience. I can fix any car.

Solomon: Any car? But I'm a super. Can you fix a kitchen sink?

Caller: A kitchen sink? No, but I can fix a Toyota.

Solomon: Thank you for calling, but I need someone with building experience.

A Friendly Assistant

Get Ready to Read

A Discuss with a partner.

1. What does a good assistant do?
2. Solomon hired an assistant. Is his life easy now?

B Match the words with the pictures.

_e_ **1.** recipe

____ **2.** "Would you like . . . ?"

____ **3.** glad

____ **4.** broken

____ **5.** heavy

____ **6.** helpful

a.

b.

c.

d.

e.

f.

🎧 *In the last episode ...*

Solomon's wife, Virginia, is angry because Solomon never has time for his family. He's very busy in the building. He goes to his boss, Mr. Morgan, and asks for an assistant. Later, he hires Bobby Crespo, a 21-year-old, to be his new assistant.

It's two weeks later, and Solomon is in Mrs. Clark's apartment. He's fixing the sink. Bobby Crespo, his assistant, is talking to Mrs. Clark. Bobby is sitting at the kitchen table with her, and Mrs. Clark is making coffee and putting a coffee cake on the table.

"**Would you like** some coffee, Bobby?" asks Mrs. Clark.

"No, thank you, Mrs. Clark," says Bobby. "I'm working."

"Are you sure, Bobby?"

"Well, just a little bit. I can work and drink coffee at the same time."

"Good. And here's some cake. I know that you love my coffee cake."

"It's delicious, Mrs. Clark," says Bobby. "Could I have the **recipe** for my mother? I told her about your delicious cake."

"Well, thank you, Bobby," says Mrs. Clark with a big smile on her face. "Of course I'll give you the recipe."

Solomon is working on the sink. The sink is **leaking**, and Solomon is getting wet.

"Bobby, could you help me here?"

"Sure, Mr. Soriano. What do you need?"

"Could you hold this **wrench** and . . ."

Bobby isn't looking at Solomon. He's looking at Mrs. Clark. She's picking up two **heavy** bottles of water. "Oh, Mrs. Clark. Don't pick up those heavy bottles. I'll do it for you. You'll hurt yourself."

"Thank you, Bobby. You're so nice. Have another piece of cake."

leak

wrench

Episode 3: A Friendly Assistant 19

Suddenly, water from the sink goes all over the floor. Solomon is very **wet**.

"Mr. Soriano, do you need some help?" Bobby asks.

"Yes, I do!" yells Solomon. Solomon stops the leaking water. "There. I fixed it."

"You're a great plumber, Mr. Soriano," says Bobby. "I'm **glad** that I'm working with you."

"I'm glad, too," says Mrs. Clark. "You're so helpful, Bobby. And you, too, Mr. Soriano. You fixed the sink!"

"No problem, Mrs. Clark," says Solomon. His clothes are wet. He's **frowning** because he's angry.

wet

The next day, Solomon is in Apartment 4D. It's the apartment of a young couple, the DeVicos. Mrs. DeVico is holding her baby, Johnny, who is crying. Solomon is standing on a **ladder** in the living room. The living room light is **broken**. Solomon is trying to fix the light, but it's difficult. He needs some help, and Bobby is late. Solomon calls Bobby on the cell phone, but 30 minutes later, Bobby isn't there.

frown

Then, the doorbell rings. It's Bobby, and he's 45 minutes late, but he's happy.

"Good morning, Mrs. DeVico. How are you? And, Johnny, how are you?"

Bobby takes Johnny in his arms, and Johnny stops crying.

"You're very good with Johnny, Bobby," says Mrs. DeVico. "Could you **hold** him for a few more minutes?"

"Oh, sure, Mrs. DeVico. Good morning, Mr. Soriano. How are you today? Do you need any help?"

"Yes, I do, Bobby. Can you . . ."

Bobby is playing with Johnny. "Come on, Johnny," says Bobby, "let's watch TV."

ladder

That evening at dinner, Solomon is very quiet. Virginia asks, "What's wrong, honey?"

"It's Bobby."

hold/carry

"Bobby? I like him, Daddy," says Susana. "He's friendly, and he talks to me all the time. We like the same music and the same movies, and . . ."

"I'm not talking about music and movies," says Solomon. "Bobby's not helping me."

"What do you mean, Solomon?" asks Virginia.

"I need an assistant. Bobby's not **helpful**. He's always late. Today he was 45 minutes late. He can't fix anything. He only watches me. He can give me the **tools**, but he can't use the tools. He makes mistakes. I told him to go to Apartment 3F and **paint** the living room. He went to Apartment 4G and painted the kitchen!"

tools

"Give him a chance, Solomon," says Virginia. "Bobby's young, but he's very friendly. I'm sure that he can do a good job. He's very helpful to me and the other tenants. He always helps me with my groceries when I come back from the supermarket. He plays basketball with Samuel and Steven after school, and everyone in the building really likes him."

"OK, I'll give him two more weeks."

paint

Reading Comprehension

A Circle *True* or *False*.

1.	Bobby is very friendly.	True	False
2.	Mrs. Clark likes Bobby.	True	False
3.	Solomon is working hard.	True	False
4.	Bobby is working hard, too.	True	False
5.	The bathroom sink is leaking.	True	False
6.	Bobby is very helpful to Solomon.	True	False
7.	Solomon holds the baby.	True	False

B Circle the correct answer.

1. Solomon is _____ .

   a. hungry   **b.** happy   **c.** unhappy

2. At Mrs. Clark's apartment, Solomon is working hard. What **isn't** Bobby doing?

   a. He isn't talking to Mrs. Clark.

   b. He isn't helping Solomon.

   c. He isn't drinking coffee.

3. Why does Susana like Bobby?

   a. He's a good assistant for her father.

   b. He plays basketball with her.

   c. Bobby and Susana like the same music and movies.

C What do people say about Bobby?

1. Write the sentences under the correct person's name.

He's helpful.	He's friendly.
He's always late.	He plays with the children.
He can't fix anything.	He's not helpful.

Virginia	Solomon

2. Write one more good point Virginia says about Bobby.

_____

_____

3. Write one more bad point Solomon says about Bobby.

_____

_____

Work with the Words

A Circle the correct answer.

1. Mrs. Clark is giving Bobby the **recipe** for her coffee cake. She is giving Bobby _____.
   a. instructions   **b.** a book   **c.** a cake

2. The sink is **leaking**. What other thing leaks?
   a. a bathtub   **b.** a TV   **c.** a cake

3. The light is **broken**. The opposite of _broken_ is _____.
   a. big   **b.** small   **c.** fixed

4. Bobby is **glad** that he's working with Solomon. Bobby is _____.
   a. happy   **b.** sad   **c.** not interested

5. What is **heavy**?
   a. a piece of paper   **b.** a car   **c.** a dollar

6. Who is **helpful**?

   a.   **b.**   **c.**

B   Read the question. Then write three more questions in your own words.

Mrs. Clark asks, "**Would you like** some coffee, Bobby?"

Would you like _____?

Would you like _____?

Would you like _____?

Lifeskill Practice

Use *Could* for requests.

We use *could* to ask for something, or to ask someone to do something.

> Bobby says, "This cake is delicious. **Could** I have the recipe for my mother?"

> Mrs. DeVico says, "You're very good with Johnny. **Could** you hold him for a few minutes?"

The answer is often "Sure!" or "Of course!"

Practice with a partner. Use the phrases from the box.

open the window	go home early
get up for a minute	get a drink of water
give me your book	ask a question
tell me the time	use the phone

A: Could you give me a pencil?   **B:** Could I have a cup of coffee?
B: Sure!   **A:** Of course!

Dialogue Practice

Practice the conversation with a classmate.

Mrs. Clark: Would you like some coffee, Bobby?

Bobby: No, thank you, Mrs. Clark. I'm working.

Mrs. Clark: Are you sure, Bobby?

Bobby: Well, just a little bit. I can work and drink coffee at the same time.

Mrs. Clark: Good. And here's some cake. I know that you love my coffee cake.

Bobby: It's delicious, Mrs. Clark. Could I have the recipe for my mother? I told her about your delicious cake.

Mrs. Clark: Well, thank you, Bobby. Of course I'll give you the recipe.

Two More Weeks

Get Ready to Read

A Discuss with a partner.

1. Why do the people in Solomon's building like Bobby?
2. Do you think Bobby will lose his job?

B Match the words with the definitions.

_c_ 1. repair   a. make someone leave his or her job

___ 2. lazy   b. use time

___ 3. polite   c. fix

___ 4. disappointed   d. not like to work

___ 5. fire   e. kind; nice; says "Please" and "Thank you"

___ 6. spend time

     f. feel sad about something that happened or didn't happen

In the last episode ...

Solomon is worried about his new assistant, Bobby Crespo. Everyone in the building likes Bobby. He's friendly, he's talkative, and he carries heavy groceries. Bobby has one problem—he's not good at his job. He can't fix leaky faucets or broken lights. He can't **repair** cabinets. He can't repair broken locks, and he's always late. He's a terrible assistant. Solomon has a problem. What is he going to do about Bobby? Solomon's wife, Virginia, says, "Give him a chance." Solomon is giving Bobby another chance. He's giving him two more weeks.

It's almost the end of the two weeks, and Bobby is very friendly to all of the tenants. Everyone likes him, but Bobby is **lazy**, too. When Solomon and Bobby go to an apartment, Bobby doesn't work. He isn't helpful to Solomon. He **spends** the **time** talking to the tenants. Bobby and the tenants have coffee and listen to the radio, and sometimes Bobby plays video games with the younger children in the building, but Bobby doesn't help Solomon. Solomon is not happy.

Now, Solomon has another problem. His daughter, Susana, likes Bobby very much. When Bobby is in the building, Susana wants to go with her father to the different apartments where he is working. Before Bobby came to work with Solomon, Susana was never interested in her father's work. Now, she wants to visit Solomon at work because she wants to see Bobby. Bobby is 21, and Susana is 16. She thinks Bobby is cute and fun. Solomon's wife, Virginia, likes Bobby because he is very **polite**. He always says, "Good morning, Mrs. Soriano. How are you today?" "Yes, ma'am," "No, ma'am," and "Can I help you?" Virginia thinks that Bobby is a nice young man.

It's the end of Bobby's second week, and Solomon and Virginia are sitting in the kitchen having a cup of coffee. The boys are in bed, and Susana is in her room doing her homework.

"I'm going to **fire** Bobby," says Solomon.

"Fire him? Why? Are the two weeks finished?" asks Virginia.

"Yes, and I gave him a chance. First, he painted the wrong apartment. Then, he broke a **faucet**. I asked him to fix a lock, and he broke it! I need to buy a new lock! And he never helps me. Virginia, I gave him two more weeks, but Bobby's terrible! He isn't helping me! Bobby gives me more work!"

"OK, but I'll be sorry to see him go. He's a nice young man. Susana is going to be very **disappointed**."

faucet

"I know. She's going to be angry, too. I think she really likes him. I'll tell her right now."

Solomon calls his daughter, "Susana!"

"What is it, Daddy? I'm studying for a test."

"Susana, I have to talk to you about something. I know that you like Bobby."

"Like him? Well, he's nice. He always helps Mom and Mrs. Clark. He's really nice."

"That's great, sweetie, but I need an assistant who can help me. I'm sorry, but I'm going to fire Bobby."

"Fire Bobby? You can't!"

"Yes, I can, Susana. This is my job, and I need help. Bobby doesn't do anything to help me."

"But everybody likes him! Mom, tell him!"

Virginia puts her arm around Susana. "Honey, your father's right. Bobby is a nice young man, but your father needs help. Anyway, Bobby's too old for you. We want you to spend more time with us."

"Well, I don't want to spend any more time with you. I want to spend time with Bobby, and he's not too old for me!" Susana runs out of the room and **slams** her bedroom door.

"Susana! Open that door!" shouts Virginia.

"It's OK," says Solomon. "In a few days, she'll forget all about Bobby."

slam

The next day, Bobby comes to work about 30 minutes late. Solomon is waiting for him. "Bobby, could you come into my office, please?"

"Sure, Mr. Soriano. How are you today? It's a beautiful day, isn't it?"

"Yes, it is, Bobby." They sit down. "Bobby, I'm sorry, but this is not working. You're always late. You never help me. You can't repair anything. I'm sorry, Bobby. Everyone in the building likes you, and you're very friendly, but I need an assistant who can help me. You're fired."

Bobby looks very sad. "I'm sorry, Mr. Soriano. I loved this job. Thank you for everything. Please tell everyone that I said good-bye."

Bobby leaves the office and leaves the building.

Reading Comprehension

A Circle *True* or *False*.

1. All the tenants like Bobby.	True	False
2. Bobby fixes everything.	True	False
3. Bobby is lazy.	True	False
4. Susana and Bobby are both 21.	True	False
5. Susana is interested in Bobby.	True	False
6. Susana wants to go to work with Solomon.	True	False
7. Susana likes Bobby because he works hard.	True	False

B Circle the correct answer.

1. Bobby made many mistakes _____.
   a. with Susana's homework
   b. in Solomon's apartment
   c. in the building

2. Solomon has to buy a new lock because _____.
   a. he broke it   **b.** Bobby broke it   **c.** a tenant broke it

3. Susana is angry at _____.
   a. her father   **b.** her mother   **c.** Bobby

C Complete the sentences with the name of the correct person.

Bobby	Solomon	Susana	Virginia

1. _____ can repair leaky faucets.

2. _____ is disappointed and angry.

3. _____ is helpful to her husband.

4. _____ is lazy but friendly.

Work with the Words

A Circle the correct answer.

1. He's not a good worker. He's very _____.
   - **a.** disappointed
   - **b.** cute
   - **c.** lazy

2. The faucet is _____.
   - **a.** leaky
   - **b.** disappointed
   - **c.** cute

3. When Susana is angry, she _____ the door.
   - **a.** slams
   - **b.** knocks on
   - **c.** repairs

4. I really wanted that job. When I didn't get it, I was very _____.
   - **a.** disappointed
   - **b.** glad
   - **c.** nervous

5. My son is very polite. He always _____.
   - **a.** works hard
   - **b.** says "Please"
   - **c.** does his homework

6. A superintendent _____ leaky faucets.
   - **a.** buys
   - **b.** repairs
   - **c.** breaks

7. The boss is going to _____ John because he is always late.
   - **a.** thank
   - **b.** pay
   - **c.** fire

B   Solomon wants to *spend* more *time* at home with his family. Where do you spend time? Complete the sentences.

In the morning, I spend time at _____.

On weekday evenings, I spend time at _____.

On weekends, I like to spend time at _____.

C   Bobby makes a lot of mistakes. Solomon says, "He can't fix anything." What *can* or *can't* you do? Check (✔) your answers.

	Yes, I can.	No, I can't.
1. Can you speak English very well?	✔	____
2. Can you understand American TV?	____	____
3. Can you read the newspaper in English?	____	____
4. Can you drive?	____	____
5. Can you dance?	____	____
6. Can you cook well?	____	____
7. Can you fix a car?	____	____
8. Can you fix a kitchen sink?	____	____

Lifeskill Practice

Use *can/can't* for ability.

Pronunciation often tells us the difference between *can* and *can't*.

I can **fix** a car. (one strong syllable)
I **can't fix** a kitchen sink. (two strong syllables)

Read the phrases below. Tell a classmate about things you *can* and *can't* do.

drive a car / fix a car
run / run very fast
speak English / speak Spanish / speak Chinese
understand American television / read American newspapers
cook for my family / cook in a restaurant / cook for 100 people

Dialogue Practice

Practice the conversation with two classmates.

Solomon: Susana!

Susana: What is it, Daddy? I'm studying for a test.

Solomon: Susana, I have to talk to you about something. I know that you like Bobby.

Susana: Like him? Well, he's nice. He always helps Mom and Mrs. Clark. He's really nice.

Solomon: That's great, sweetie, but I need an assistant who can help me. I'm sorry, but I'm going to fire Bobby.

Susana: Fire Bobby? You can't!

Solomon: Yes, I can, Susana. This is my job, and I need help. Bobby doesn't do anything to help me.

Susana: But everybody likes him! Mom, tell him!

Virginia: Honey, your father's right. Bobby is a nice young man, but your father needs help. Anyway, Bobby's too old for you. We want you to spend more time with us.

Susana: Well, I don't want to spend any more time with you. I want to spend time with Bobby, and he's not too old for me!

Virginia: Susana! Open that door!

Solomon: It's OK. In a few days, she'll forget all about Bobby.

The Next Assistant

Get Ready to Read

A Discuss with a partner.

1. Why isn't Bobby working for Solomon?
2. What kind of assistant does Solomon need?

B Match the words with the definitions.

_e_ 1. improve   **a.** think hard

____ 2. mad   **b.** feel sad about something or someone who is not here

____ 3. miss

____ 4. another   **c.** the response when you hear bad news

____ 5. "I'm sorry to hear that."   **d.** angry

____ 6. concentrate   **e.** do better; get better

       f. one more

In the last episode ...

Solomon gives Bobby Crespo two weeks to improve, but Bobby doesn't improve. He doesn't help Solomon make repairs in the apartments. Finally, Solomon fires Bobby. Solomon's daughter, Susana, is angry at her father because she likes Bobby, but Solomon needs someone to help him in the building.

The next day, Solomon goes to his boss's office again. He tells Mr. Morgan about Bobby. "**I'm sorry to hear that**, Solomon," says Mr. Morgan. "We'll put **another** ad in the paper, but this is the last one. The ads are expensive!"

"Thank you, Mr. Morgan."

On Saturday, there's another ad in the paper.

A few days later, Solomon hires another assistant. His name is Thomas Fontana. He's about 49 and married with four children. He works as a security guard in an office building at night, but he needs extra money for his children's college **tuition**.*

Solomon asks, "Can you start tomorrow, Tom?"

"It's Thomas," he answers. "Tomorrow? Yes, I can start tomorrow. What time?"

"Can you start at 8 o'clock?" asks Solomon.

Thomas thinks for a minute. "Eight? No, I can't. I sleep in the morning. I can start at two."

"Two? That's a little late, and I'm usually busy in the morning, but OK. I need the help."

"OK, Mr. Soriano. See you at two tomorrow."

"See you at two, Tom," says Solomon.

"Thomas. Call me Thomas," answers Thomas.

"I'm sorry. See you tomorrow, Thomas."

It's dinnertime a week later, and Solomon and his family are sitting down at the kitchen table. They're getting ready to eat.

*tuition = the money you pay for school

"It's so nice to sit down and eat with the family," says Solomon, "and tomorrow I'm going to Stevie and Sam's baseball game. Life is **improving**! But where's Susana?"

Steven answers, "She's in her room on her computer."

"Why isn't she eating with us?" asks Solomon.

Samuel laughs, "She's still **mad** at you, Dad. You fired Bobby. She's not talking to you."

Steven says, "Yeah, Dad. You're in big trouble."

Virginia adds, "Be quiet, you two, and eat your dinner. Solomon, don't worry about Susana. She's 16. She'll start talking to you again in a few days."

"I hope so. I **miss** talking to her," says Solomon. "Let's eat. Please pass the potatoes."

They're eating **dessert*** when the telephone rings. It's Mrs. Clark.

"Good evening, Mr. Soriano. Could you come up here, please? My dishwasher isn't working."

"Someone will be up in a few minutes, Mrs. Clark," answers Solomon. Solomon calls Thomas's cell phone, and he sits down at the table with his family. "Finally, I can eat my dinner."

A few minutes later, Thomas is at Mrs. Clark's apartment door. He rings the doorbell.

"Just a minute," says Mrs. Clark. She opens the door and says, "Who are you?"

"I'm Thomas Fontana. I'm Mr. Soriano's new assistant."

"Where's Bobby?"

"Bobby who?"

"You don't know Bobby? He works in this building, too. He's a very nice young man. He visits me every afternoon, but I haven't seen him this week."

"I don't know Bobby. Where's the dishwasher?" Thomas is still standing in the hallway.

"Oh, I'm sorry. Come in. Come in. Would you like a cup of coffee?"

"No, thank you. I want to start working."

"How about some coffee cake? It's very good."

"No, thank you. I don't eat **sweets**."**

"No sweets? Oh, that's too bad. I make delicious sweets."

***dessert** = something sweet after a meal (can be fruit)
****sweets** = cake, cookies, pie, candy (not fruit)

Thomas is opening the dishwasher and looking inside. He isn't looking at Mrs. Clark. "Excuse me, but I have to **concentrate** when I work. I can't talk to you now." He takes out his tools and begins to work.

"Oh, well, I'll go in the living room, then." Mrs. Clark walks out of the kitchen and goes to the living room.

Reading Comprehension

A Circle *True* or *False*.

1. Bobby's work improved.	True	False
2. Susana is angry at Solomon.	True	False
3. Mr. Morgan wants to have many ads.	True	False
4. Thomas Fontana knows Bobby.	True	False
5. Thomas has two jobs now.	True	False
6. Thomas can work early in the morning.	True	False

B Circle the correct answer.

1. What time does Solomon usually begin work?
   a. 8:00 A.M.   **b.** 2:00 P.M.   **c.** 11:00 A.M.

2. Where is Susana at dinnertime?
   a. in the kitchen   **b.** at school   **c.** in her room

3. Solomon is _____ because Susana is angry.
   a. happy   **b.** sad   **c.** nervous

C   Put the following sentences in order from 1 to 7.

_____ Thomas starts working for Solomon.

_____ Solomon fires Bobby.

_____ Solomon hires Bobby.

__1__ Mr. Morgan puts the first ad in the newspaper.

_____ Bobby doesn't do a good job.

_____ Solomon hires Thomas.

_____ Mr. Morgan puts another ad in the newspaper.

Work with the Words

A   Circle the correct answer.

1. Bobby didn't **improve**, so Solomon fired him. "My English is improving" means _____.
   a. it's getting better   b. it's getting worse   c. it's the same

2. When is NOT a good time to **concentrate**?
   a. when you are working   b. during a test   c. when you want to sleep

3. Mr. Morgan says "I'm sorry to hear that" when Solomon tells him about Bobby. A good time to answer "I'm sorry to hear that" is when you hear: _____.
   a. "My wife just had a baby"   b. "I feel sick today."   c. "I have a new job."

4. Linda is **mad**. She _____ .
   a. lost her money   b. got invited to a party   c. did well on her test

5. Susana misses _____.
   a. Bobby   b. her father   c. her brothers

6. Thomas doesn't eat **sweets**. Which is NOT a sweet?

a.    **b.**    **c.**

B   Complete the sentences with *a, an,* or *another.*

1. Solomon fired Bobby. Now he needs _____ assistant.
2. That coffee cake was so delicious! Could I have _____ piece?
3. Good morning! Here's _____ cup of coffee.
4. Could I have _____ apple?
5. Please sit down. Would you like _____ glass of water?

Lifeskill Practice

When we hear bad news, we often say, "I'm sorry to hear that." For good news, we say "Congratulations"!

A   Practice the conversations.

A: I just got a new job.
B: Congratulations!

A: I lost my job.
B: I'm sorry to hear that.

B   Student A, give some good news or bad news. Student B, Say "I'm sorry to hear that" or "Congratulations!"

Examples:

"I lost my wallet."

"My sister just had a baby."

"I got a promotion."

"I didn't pass my driving test."

Dialogue Practice

Practice the conversation with a classmate.

Mrs. Clark: Who are you?

Thomas: I'm Thomas Fontana. I'm Mr. Soriano's new assistant.

Mrs. Clark: Where's Bobby?

Thomas: Bobby who?

Mrs. Clark: You don't know Bobby? He works in this building, too. He's a very nice young man. He visits me every afternoon, but I haven't seen him this week.

Thomas: I don't know Bobby. Where's the dishwasher?

Mrs. Clark: Oh, I'm sorry. Come in. Come in. Would you like a cup of coffee?

Thomas: No, thank you. I want to start working.

Mrs. Clark: How about some coffee cake? It's very good.

Thomas: No, thank you. I don't eat sweets.

Mrs. Clark: No sweets? Oh, that's too bad. I make delicious sweets.

Thomas: Excuse me, but I have to concentrate when I work. I can't talk to you now.

Mrs. Clark: Oh, well, I'll go in the living room, then.

Thomas on the Job

Get Ready to Read

A   Discuss with a partner.

1. How is Thomas different from Bobby?
2. Will the tenants like Thomas?

B   Match the words with their opposites.

___f___ 1. impolite   **a.** happy to be alone

_____ 2. lonely   **b.** say good things

_____ 3. shy   **c.** quiet

_____ 4. in a good mood **d.** friendly, wanting to talk to other people

_____ 5. complain   **e.** angry

_____ 6. talkative   **f.** polite

In the last episode ...

Solomon fires his assistant Bobby Crespo. Now he has a new assistant, Thomas, who is older and more experienced. Solomon is happy because Thomas is good at fixing things in the building, and Solomon has more time with his family. But Mrs. Clark misses Bobby because Thomas is not friendly or talkative.

Ring, ring! Ring, ring! The Soriano's telephone is ringing.

"I'll get it!" yells Steven. "Hello? Just a minute. Dad, it's for you!"

"Thanks, Stevie," says Solomon. "Hello? Hello, Mrs. Clark. How can I help you today? Oh, really, Mrs. Clark? I understand, Mrs. Clark. That's true. He is different from Bobby, but he's a good worker. No, he doesn't eat sweets, Mrs. Clark. Mm, hmm. I understand, Mrs. Clark, but is your light working? It is? Good. I'll talk to him, Mrs. Clark. Maybe he'll be more **talkative**. Well, **I've got to go.*** Good-bye."

talkative

"What did she want?" asks Virginia.

"She was **complaining** about Thomas. She calls me every day."

"You know, Solomon, other tenants complain to me, too. They don't like Thomas. He never talks to the tenants. He's not friendly or talkative."

"I know, Virginia, but Thomas is a really good assistant. I can eat dinner with the family now, and I went to the boys' baseball game last week. I have much more free time."

"Well, that's true," says Virginia, "but all the tenants liked Bobby because he played with the children, helped carry groceries, and talked to the elderly tenants. You know, Mrs. Clark loved to talk to Bobby. I think she misses him."

"I'm sorry about that, but Bobby didn't fix anything! Sure, he was friendly, but I need an assistant who can fix things. Thomas can fix anything."

"I know. I know. Maybe he's a little **shy**. Some people need more time to make friends," says Virginia.

"You're right. Maybe he's shy."

A few weeks later, Virginia is in the laundry room talking to a close friend, Belinda, who also lives in the building. She has a 16-year-old daughter named Paulette, and Susana and Paulette are best friends.

***I've got to go.** = *I have to leave now.* Or *I have to stop talking now.*

"Belinda, did you see Mrs. Clark today?" asks Virginia.

"No, I didn't. She usually does laundry with me on Wednesdays, and then we have coffee. But she's not here today."

"I hope she's OK. I think she's a little **lonely**. She misses Bobby, and she doesn't like Thomas, Solomon's new assistant. She likes to see Solomon, but he doesn't have time to visit. He's spending more time at home and at the boys' baseball games."

"That's great for you, Virginia, but I don't like Thomas either."

"Why not?"

"I don't know. I'm uncomfortable when he's in my apartment. He's not very friendly, and he never talks."

"Maybe he's shy."

"Shy? No. He's not nice. I gave him a glass of water, and he didn't even say 'Thank you.' That's very **impolite**."

"Really? Well, there are a lot of complaints about Thomas. Solomon doesn't like him very much either, but Thomas is very good at fixing things in the building."

Suddenly, Susana comes into the laundry room. "Hi, Aunt Belinda. Hi, Mom!"

"Hi, sweetie. Did you finish your homework?" asks Virginia.

"Yes, I did. **May I*** go to the mall with Paulette? We want to go to the movies."

"To the mall? How are you going to get there?" asks Belinda.

"Dad's going to drive us." Susana answers.

"OK, but call us as soon as the movie is over," Virginia says. "Dad or I will **pick** you **up**."**

"Thanks, Mom. Bye, Aunt Belinda!" Susana runs out the door.

Virginia and Belinda watch Susana leave. "Well, she's **in a good mood** today," says Belinda.

"Yeah, she is. For about ten days she was very mad at Solomon. Now she's happy. Teenagers!"

***May I** = a polite way to ask for permission.

**Dad or I will **pick** you **up** = Dad or I will come to the mall and bring you home.

Episode 6: Thomas on the Job 45

Ring, ring! Ring, ring! Virginia's cell phone is ringing. "Excuse me, Belinda. Hello?"

"Mrs. Soriano? This is Mrs. Johnson in 5C. Could you call Mr. Soriano right away? My husband was taking a shower when all of the cold water stopped. My husband got burned by the hot water. We have no cold water!"

"Oh, my goodness! Solomon's not here, but I'll call his assistant right away!"

Reading Comprehension

A Circle *True* or *False*.

1. Mrs. Clark is upset.	True	False
2. Mrs. Clark's light is working.	True	False
3. Mrs. Clark complained about Bobby.	True	False
4. Thomas likes to talk.	True	False
5. Thomas can fix anything.	True	False
6. Solomon has more time with his family now.	True	False
7. Mrs. Clark misses Thomas.	True	False

B Circle the correct answer.

1. Virginia thinks that Thomas is _____.
   a. angry   **b.** unfriendly   **c.** shy

2. Who is Belinda?
   a. Susana's sister   **b.** Solomon's friend   **c.** Virginia's friend

3. How does Belinda feel about Thomas?
   a. She likes him.   **b.** She thinks he is nice.   **c.** She thinks he is impolite.

C Write answers to the questions.

1. Where are Virginia and Belinda? _____.

2. Where is Susana going? _____.

3. Who is she going with? _____.

4. Who is taking the girls to the mall? _____.

5. What are the girls going to do there? _____.

6. What is the problem in Mrs. Johnson's apartment? _____

_____.

Work with the Words

A Circle the correct answer.

1. Mrs. Smith is **complaining**. She says _____.
   a. "It's ten o'clock."   **b.** "We have no cold water!"   **c.** "He's very nice."

2. "I think she's a little **lonely**." She _____.
   a. doesn't have friends   **b.** lives alone   **c.** doesn't eat enough

3. "Maybe Thomas is **shy**." Thomas doesn't like _____.
   a. to work   **b.** to be with new people   **c.** to be alone

4. Susana is **in a good mood** today. She is _____.

    a. sad   **b.** angry   **c.** happy

5. Belinda thinks Thomas is **impolite**. She gave him a drink, but he didn't say _____.

    a. "Good morning"   **b.** "Thank you"   **c.** "Hello"

6. My mother is **talkative**. She is _____.

    a. quiet   **b.** loud   **c.** hungry

B Circle *True* or *False*.

1. After English class, a family member picks me up.	**True**	**False**
2. Before work, a friend picks me up.	**True**	**False**
3. After work, someone picks me up.	**True**	**False**
4. In the afternoon, I pick up my children.	**True**	**False**
5. In the morning, a school bus picks up my children.	**True**	**False**

Lifeskill Practice

Use *May I* to ask for permission.

Susana says: "**May I** go to the mall with Paulette?"

Complete the conversations and ask for permission. Use the phrases in parentheses or your own ideas.

1. Daughter: May I go to _____?
(the mall, my friend's house, the movies)

    Mother: Yes, but come home early.

2. Grandson: May I have _____?
(a cookie, $5, your coat*)

    Grandfather: Sure.

3. Student A: May I use _____?
(the phone, your pen, your dictionary)

    Student B: Sure.

May I have your coat? = May I hang up your coat for you?

Dialogue Practice

Practice the conversation with three classmates.

Susana: Hi, Aunt Belinda. Hi, Mom!

Virginia: Hi, sweetie. Did you finish your homework?

Susana: Yes, I did. May I go to the mall with Paulette? We want to go to the movies.

Belinda: To the mall? How are you going to get there?

Susana: Dad's going to drive us.

Virginia: OK, but call us as soon as the movie is over. Dad or I will pick you up.

Susana: Thanks, Mom. Bye, Aunt Belinda!

Belinda: Well, she's in a good mood today.

Virginia: Yeah, she is. For about ten days, she was very mad at Solomon. Now she's happy. Teenagers! (*Telephone rings.*) Excuse me, Belinda. Hello?

Mrs. Johnson: Mrs. Soriano? This is Mrs. Johnson in 5C. Could you call Mr. Soriano right away? My husband was taking a shower when all of the cold water stopped. My husband got burned by the hot water. We have no cold water!

Virginia: Oh, my goodness! Solomon's not here, but I'll call his assistant right away!

What's Happening in the Building?

Get Ready to Read

  Discuss with a partner.

1. What are some problems that people have in their apartments?

leaks

mice

leaky dishwasher

broken lock

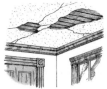

falling plaster

cockroaches

2. What problems can a super fix? Is Soloman always happy to fix problems?

B Match the words with the sentences.

_b_ **1.** fussy   **a.** "I can't do this. It's very difficult for me."

_____ **2.** frustrated   **b.** "You're doing it wrong! Do it again."

_____ **3.** tip   **c.** "You did great work. Here's a little extra money for you."

_____ **4.** thankful

_____ **5.** worried   **d.** "She didn't call! She's only 16, and I don't know where she is!"

_____ **6.** confused

    e. "Thank you very much."

    f. "I don't understand."

There are a lot of problems in the building. Many of the tenants don't like Thomas because he's not friendly or talkative. Mrs. Clark misses the other assistant, Bobby. Virginia's friend Belinda doesn't feel comfortable around Thomas. But Solomon thinks that Thomas is a good assistant, and he likes him. Susana and Belinda's daughter, Paulette, are going to the mall to see a movie. Virginia is going to pick them up after the movie.

"Thank you very much," says Mrs. Johnson. "You were very helpful. Here. Take this." She gives Thomas an **envelope** of money.

envelope

"I'm sorry, Mrs. Johnson," says Thomas, "but I can't accept that. This is my job."

"It's just a little **tip**," she says. "I want to thank you for your help. You came right away and fixed the pipes. My husband is very **thankful**. We're going to tell Mr. Soriano everything."

Thomas takes the envelope from Mrs. Johnson. "Thank you, Mrs. Johnson. If you have any more trouble, please call Mr. Soriano."

"I'm going to call *you*, Thomas."

Thomas is walking to the stairs when Solomon comes running up.

"What happened, Thomas? I got your message, and I was so **worried**! Is everything OK? I was driving Susana and her friend to the mall, and the traffic was terrible."

"Everything is fine, Mr. Soriano," answers Thomas. "Now the Johnsons have cold and hot water."

"Is Mrs. Johnson upset? She's very **fussy**. The work has to be perfect."

"She's very happy. I didn't have any trouble, and the **pipes** are working fine."

pipes

"The pipes? I fixed those pipes last month. I can't believe that there was a problem again."

"Well, everything is working now."

"Thanks, Thomas. You did a great job."

Solomon goes back to his apartment and checks his messages. There are four messages from tenants. In Apartment 5A there's a **leaky faucet**, and there's water all over the bathroom. Solomon fixed the faucet a month ago. Downstairs in Apartment 4A, the water from 5A is leaking into the bathroom, so Solomon and Thomas have to fix the bathroom ceiling, too. Later, Solomon and Thomas go to Apartment 2D, Mr. Jackson's apartment. He's an elderly tenant, and he never complains, but today he's angry. He wants to watch his favorite TV program, but the electricity isn't working in the living room. Solomon doesn't understand it. He fixed the **socket** two weeks ago. Solomon is very **frustrated** and **confused** because he always checks his repairs. He thinks "What's happening in this building?" He and Thomas spend the rest of the day fixing the problems.

leaky faucet

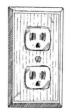

socket

Solomon is in an apartment fixing another leaky faucet when Susana calls. "Dad, could you pick us up? The movie is over."

"I'm sorry, honey, I'm very busy. Your mother will pick you up. Wait outside the movie theater." Solomon calls Virginia, and a few minutes later she drives over to the mall. When she arrives, she sees Susana and Paulette talking to a boy. She thinks, "He looks like Bobby Crespo." Then she says,

"That *is* Bobby!" Virginia stops in front of the theater, and Susana, Paulette, and Bobby walk over to the car.

"Mom, look who was at the mall! We saw Bobby after the movie was over." Susana has a big smile on her face.

"Hello, Mrs. Soriano. How are you?" asks Bobby.

"I'm fine, thank you, Bobby. It's nice to see you again."

"How's Mr. Soriano?"

"He's fine, thank you. Come on, girls. My dinner is on the stove and Sam and Stevie are watching it. Let's go! Bye, Bobby!"

Susana smiles and says, "Bye, Bobby!"

"Bye, Mrs. Soriano. Bye, Susana. Nice to meet you, Paulette."

Later that evening, Virginia, Solomon, and the children are finishing dinner. Solomon looks terrible, and he's in a bad mood. The telephone rang four times during dinner.

"Honey, you look terrible. Go to bed," says Virginia.

"I can't. I don't know what's going on. I never had so many problems before. I'm lucky that I have Thomas. He's great. No one is complaining about him now because he's very good at his job. He helped me a lot today. And he isn't shy. He's quiet. I just don't understand what's going on here." Suddenly, Susana's cell phone rings.

"Hey! No cell phones at the dinner table!" yells Solomon.

"I'm sorry, Dad," says Susana. "It's just Paulette." She looks at her phone, reads a text message, and smiles.

Reading Comprehension

A   Circle *True* or *False*.

1. Mrs. Johnson is upset with Thomas.	**True**	**False**
2. Thomas does a good job for the Johnsons.	**True**	**False**
3. Thomas takes the money from Mrs. Johnson.	**True**	**False**
4. There are no problems in the building.	**True**	**False**
5. Solomon broke some pipes.	**True**	**False**
6. Solomon is very busy.	**True**	**False**
7. Everyone is complaining about Thomas.	**True**	**False**

B   Circle the correct answer.

1. How many apartments have problems?
   a. one   **b.** two   **c.** more than three

2. Who do Susana and Paulette meet at the mall?
   a. Susana's brothers   **b.** Thomas   **c.** Bobby

3. Solomon likes Thomas because he is _____.
   a. good at the job   **b.** friendly   **c.** not helpful

C   Who said it? Read each sentence. Write the name of the correct person.

Bobby	Mrs. Johnson	Solomon	Susana	Virginia

_____ **1.** "I was so worried!"

_____ **2.** "Nice to meet you, Paulette."

_____ **3.** "My dinner is on the stove and Sam and Stevie are watching it."

_____ **4.** "Could you pick us up?"

_____ **5.** "No cell phones at the dinner table!"

_____ **6.** "It's just a little tip."

_____ **7.** "I don't know what's going on."

Work with the Words

Circle the correct answer.

1. Which word means "extra money"?

   a. tip   **b.** faucet   **c.** socket

2. Who gets **tips** at work?

   a. a waitress   **b.** a teacher   **c.** a doctor

3. I am **thankful** for _____.

   a. heavy traffic   **b.** my bad boss   **c.** my family

4. She's **fussy**. She _____.

   a. never does her homework

   b. does her homework in three minutes

   c. does her homework three times to get it perfect

5. Electricity comes from the _____.

   a. pipes   **b.** socket   **c.** faucet

6. Who is **frustrated**?

   a. a person who has a new car

   b. an excellent student

   c. a person in a foreign country who can't speak the country's language

7. Solomon is **confused** about what's happening in his building. When is a student **confused**?

   a. when he or she understands everything

   b. when he or she does poorly on a test

   c. when he or she is a very good student

Lifeskill Practice

■ Here are some ways to talk about electricity in your home.

Match the sentences with the pictures.

_____ **1.** The socket is broken.

_____ **2.** Unplug it.

_____ **3.** The socket is full.

_____ **4.** Plug it in.

a. 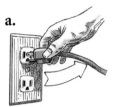 b. 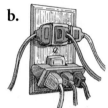 c.  d.

Dialogue Practice

Practice the conversation with two classmates.

Susana: Mom, look who was at the mall! We saw Bobby after the movie was over.

Bobby: Hello, Mrs. Soriano. How are you?

Virginia: I'm fine, thank you, Bobby. It's nice to see you again.

Bobby: How's Mr. Soriano?

Virginia: He's fine, thank you. Come on, girls. My dinner is on the stove and Sam and Stevie are watching it. Let's go! Bye, Bobby!

Susana: Bye, Bobby!

Bobby: Bye, Mrs. Soriano. Bye, Susana. Nice to meet you, Paulette.

Trouble for Solomon

Get Ready to Read

A   Discuss with a partner.

1. Who sends Susana a message on her cell phone?
2. What do you think Solomon is going to do?

B   Match each sentence with the sentence that has the same meaning.

_c_   1. He is **seeing** her.

____   2. He looks **familiar**.

____   3. He's going to **quit** his job.

____   4. He is **suspicious**.

____   5. He is getting a **raise**.

____   6. He's **moving out**.

a. He is getting more money at work.

b. He thinks something is not right.

c. He is dating her.

d. He's going to live at a different address.

e. I know his face.

f. He's going to to leave his job.

In the last episode ...

There are many problems in the building. The tenants are angry. They think that Solomon can't fix anything, so they are calling Thomas when they have problems in their apartments.

Yesterday Mr. Morgan called, so today Solomon is sitting in Mr. Morgan's office. He's early, so he's waiting for ten o'clock. On the telephone, Mr. Morgan was **furious**!* Solomon is worried. "What am I going to do? Is Mr. Morgan going to fire me? I have three children and a wife to take care of. I can't lose my job!" Then the office door opens, and another man comes out of the office with Mr. Morgan. They are laughing, and Mr. Morgan isn't angry. At first, the other man isn't **familiar** to Solomon. He doesn't know him. Then Solomon says to himself, "That's Thomas! What's he doing here?" Thomas is wearing a suit. He never wears a suit, and he never smiles, but he's smiling now.

"Thank you, Thomas," says Mr. Morgan. "I'll call you later. It was very nice to meet you."

"It was nice to meet you, too, Mr. Morgan," says Thomas. "Thank you very much."

"Come in, Solomon," says Mr. Morgan. He isn't smiling now.

Solomon slowly walks into Mr. Morgan's office. They sit down.

"Solomon, there are serious problems at 112 Standish. This is not good. Tenants are complaining, and some tenants want to **move out** of the building.

"I know, Mr. Morgan. It's terrible, but I don't understand it. We never had problems like this before."

"Well, I don't want anyone to move out. I think you need more help."

"But I have Thomas. He's not very friendly, but he's good at fixing things."

"I know. Many tenants say that he does good work. Thomas came to the office today for an interview, and I hired him."

"You hired him? But he has another job. He works at night as a security guard."

*furious = very, very angry

"I know, but he's going to **quit** that job. I'm going to pay him more. I'm going to give him a **raise**, and he's going to work for me. He's going to work with you."

Solomon is surprised. "Full-time?" he asks.

"Yes. Full-time. Now, there will be two superintendents and a part-time assistant."

Now Solomon is confused. He asks, "A part-time assistant, too? Who?"

"Well, Thomas has a nephew who has experience working in an apartment building."

"Oh, really? What's his name?"

"Just a minute. Let me check. Oh, his name is Bob Crespo."

"Bobby Crespo? Bobby Crespo? I fired Bobby Crespo! He's Thomas's nephew?"

"Yes, that's right. Thomas said that you fired Bobby, but I'm going to give him another chance. He's going to start tomorrow morning."

"Tomorrow morning? But Bobby is no good! He can't fix anything."

"I'm sure that Thomas will help Bobby. I'm sorry, Solomon, but I have another appointment. I don't want any more complaints from the tenants. Good-bye."

"Yes, sir." Solomon walks out of the office.

Solomon goes home, but he's very angry. Now he's **suspicious** of Thomas. He's driving home and talking to himself. "Hmm. Now I understand. Thomas is working in the building because of Bobby. I think Bobby and Thomas want to control my building."

Solomon gets home and tells Virginia everything. She can't believe it. Now she has to tell Solomon some more bad news. "Solomon, I have to tell you something."

"What is it? More problems?"

"Maybe. I think Susana is **seeing** Bobby."

"What? What are you talking about?"

"Well, we didn't tell you, but last week Susana and Paulette saw Bobby at the mall."

"At the mall? Why didn't you tell me? Now I understand. Maybe Susana told Bobby about the problems in the building."

"Really? I don't think so. I think he really likes Susana, but I'm worried. She said she was at Paulette's, but I called and she's not there. I think she's with Bobby right now."

"Where is she now?"

"I think she's at the library."

Suddenly, Steven and Samuel come into the kitchen.

"Susana's not at the library. She's at the mall with Bobby. Sam heard her talking on her cell phone, but we're not supposed to say anything. She gave us $5.00, and she said we can use her computer. Is she in trouble?"

Reading Comprehension

A Circle *True* or *False*.

1. Solomon is nervous about his appointment.   True   False
2. Many tenants like Thomas now.   True   False
3. Solomon isn't worried about his job.   True   False
4. Mr. Morgan likes Thomas.   True   False
5. Solomon thinks Bobby is no good.   True   False
6. Thomas has a new job in another building.   True   False
7. Thomas will continue to work part-time.   True   False

B Circle the correct answer.

1. How many people will work at 112 Standish?
   a. one   b. two   c. three

2. Who is going to work part-time?
   a. Solomon   b. Thomas   c. Bobby

3. Why is Solomon suspicious of Thomas?
   a. because Solomon didn't need help
   b. because Bobby is not friendly
   c. because he didn't know that Bobby is Thomas's nephew

C Read each sentence. Write the name of the correct person.

Bobby	Mr. Morgan	Solomon	Thomas

_____ 1. He's furious.

_____ 2. He's not talkative.

_____ 3. He has many problems.

_____ 4. He's getting another chance.

_____ 5. He is suspicious.

_____ 6. Bobby is his nephew.

Work with the Words

A Circle the correct answer.

1. Who is **furious**?

   a.   b.   c.

2. Some of Solomon's tenants want to **move out**. Where do they want to go?

   a. to work

   b. to new apartments in his building

   c. to apartments in a different building

3. *I am **suspicious** of her* means _____.

   a. I like her

   b. I think she is hardworking

   c. I don't believe her

4. *He looks **familiar** to me* means _____.

   a. I think I know him. **b.** I like his smile.   **c.** I think he's tired.

5. *She's going to **quit** her job* means _____.

   a. She's fired.

   b. She's leaving the job, but she isn't fired.

   c. She doesn't have a new job.

6. Which employee will get a **raise**?

   a. He always arrives early and works hard.

   b. He's usually late.

   c. He calls in sick four times a month.

Lifeskill Practice

▨ We call the super about many problems in our apartment.

Ⓐ Write the name of the problem next to the picture.

a broken lock	**cockroaches**	**falling plaster**
a leaking dishwasher	**mice**	**a leaky faucet**

1. _____

2. _____

3. _____

4. _____

5. _____

6. _____

B Practice the phone conversation.

A: Hello, this is the super. What's the problem?

B: Hello, this is _____ in 4A. I have _____.

A: I'll be right there.

Dialogue Practice

Practice the conversation with two classmates.

Virginia: Solomon, I have to tell you something.

Solomon: What is it? More problems?

Virginia: Maybe. I think Susana is seeing Bobby.

Solomon: What? What are you talking about?

Virginia: Well, we didn't tell you, but last week Susana and Paulette saw Bobby at the mall.

Solomon: At the mall? Why didn't you tell me? Now I understand. Maybe Susana told Bobby about the problems in the building.

Virginia: Really? I don't think so. I think he really likes Susana, but I'm worried. She said she was at Paulette's, but I called and she's not there. I think she is with Bobby right now.

Solomon: Where is she now?

Virginia: I think she's at the library.

Steven: Susana's not at the library. She's at the mall with Bobby. Sam heard her talking on her cell phone, but we're not supposed to say anything. She gave us $5.00, and she said we can use her computer. Is she in trouble?

Solomon's Plan

Get Ready to Read

A Discuss with a partner.

1. Do you think that Thomas and Bobby want to control Solomon's building?
2. What is Solomon going to do?

B Match the words with the definitions.

_a_ 1. crowded   **a.** having a lot of people in one place

____ 2. lie   **b.** the area around an apartment or house

____ 3. honest   **c.** telling the truth

____ 4. neighborhood   **d.** money added to someone's pay,
                            especially as a reward
____ 5. bonus

____ 6. embarrass   **e.** make someone feel uncomfortable or
                            shy in public

                        f. not tell the truth

In the last episode ...

Solomon has an appointment with his boss, Mr. Morgan. Mr. Morgan is very upset about the problems in the building. Solomon is very surprised because Thomas has a new job: he's a new super in his building! Another surprise is Bobby. Thomas is Bobby's uncle! Solomon and Virginia can't believe it. They think that Bobby and Thomas want to control Solomon's building. Another problem is Bobby and Susana. Maybe Susana is seeing Bobby. Solomon knows that Susana was upset when he fired Bobby. Susana says that she is at Paulette's house, but Steven and Samuel say that Susana is at the mall with Bobby. She paid them $5.00 to be quiet.

Virginia and Solomon are in the kitchen talking about the problems. Right now, Solomon is putting on his coat. He's worried about Susana. She's at the mall with Bobby. The boys are worried that Susana will be angry at them, but Solomon says, "Don't worry, boys. I'll take care of this."

A few minutes later, Solomon is at the mall. He is looking for Susana. Solomon is furious! He doesn't want Susana to see Bobby for three reasons: First, Bobby is too old for Susana; second, Bobby is lazy and not a good worker; and finally, Bobby and his uncle, Thomas, are not **honest** people. Solomon didn't know that Bobby was Thomas's nephew, and he is suspicious of Bobby and Thomas.

Solomon is worried. He thinks: "Did Bobby and Thomas make the problems in the building? What's going on? Why are there so many problems in the building? Why did Thomas become the super? And where is Susana?"

Solomon goes to the movie theater first, but Susana and Bobby are not there. "Maybe they're at the food court," he thinks.

At first, Solomon can't find Susana. There are many tables, and the food court is **crowded** because it's Friday night. The mall is always crowded on Friday nights because many people like to go to the movie theater there. Then he sees Susana and Bobby and says, "There they are!"

Solomon is running across the food court when Susana sees him. "Uh, oh! Bobby! My father is here! I'm in big trouble."

"Susana, what are you doing here with him? You're not with Paulette! Why did you **lie** to your mother?" shouts Solomon. He's frowning and his face is getting a little red.

"Daddy, be quiet! You're **embarrassing** me! People are looking," complains Susana.

"Embarrassing you? Embarrassing you? You lied to your mother. You said that you were going to Paulette's house. I can't believe it! You usually do not lie to us."

"But, Daddy, I . . . I . . ."

"Be quiet, Susana."

Then Bobby speaks. "Mr. Soriano, I'm sorry. I was in your **neighborhood**, and I saw Susana. I invited her to the movies."

"Oh, really? That's interesting, Bobby. Today Mr. Morgan hired your uncle, Thomas, to be a new super in my building, and Mr. Morgan says that you are going to come back to work in the building."

"Oh, you know about Uncle Thomas? Well, this is great. Now we can work together again!"

"Work together? But Bobby, why do you want to come back to work in my building? You never worked hard before. You were friendly to the tenants, but you didn't help me. The building is old, and now there are many problems in the building. I have to work very hard every day."

"Problems? Oh, we can fix those problems, Mr. Soriano. Uncle Thomas only broke a few pipes and broke a light or two. He can fix everything in a few hours. He can . . ."

"What are you talking about, Bobby?" asks Susana.

"I . . . I mean . . . Uncle Thomas is good at fixing things. He can . . . He can fix all of the . . . problems." Bobby is very nervous.

"I don't understand. Daddy, what is Bobby talking about?" asks Susana. She is a little upset.

"Well, Susana," says Solomon, "this is very interesting. I think that your friend, Bobby, and his uncle, Thomas, broke some things in the building to make trouble for me. Then, many tenants complained to Mr. Morgan, so now Bobby can come back to work, and his uncle has a new full-time job."

"No! Bobby, is that true?" Susana asks.

Bobby is different now. He isn't smiling. "That's right, Mr. Soriano. My uncle and I are going to control the building and fire you! The tenants like me, and they like my uncle. You can't do anything about it!"

Solomon is smiling. He is putting his hand in his jacket pocket. In his hand, there is a small tape recorder.

"Well, Bobby, I can do something about it. Our conversation is on this tape recorder, and I'm going to play this tape for Mr. Morgan. Let's go, Susana."

"Yeah, let's go, Daddy. There's nothing interesting here."

Susana and Solomon walk away. Bobby is sitting at the table alone.

* * * *

One month later, the Soriano family is on vacation in Miami on a beautiful beach. They're enjoying the warm weather and the sun. Solomon is in a very good mood because many things changed after Mr. Morgan listened to the tape. First he fired Thomas and Bobby. Then he hired two part-time assistants for Solomon. But that's not all!

Virginia says, "Honey, this is a wonderful vacation, and we're all having a great time. Mr. Morgan was very nice to give you a two-week vacation and a **bonus**."

"You're right, but I worked very hard for this vacation. Next year, Mr. Morgan is going to give us a bigger apartment in a new building. We can take a vacation every year. Hey! Who's Susana talking to?"

"Oh, that's a very nice boy. His parents are very nice, too. Susana isn't thinking about Bobby anymore."

"No, she isn't, and I'm not thinking about him, either."

Samuel and Steven are playing in the water. "Hey, Dad, come on! The water's great! Look, Dad. Mrs. Clark is going to jump in the water. She's a lot of fun, Dad!"

Virginia gets out of her chair and says, "Come on, honey. Let's go swimming!"

Reading Comprehension

A Circle *True* or *False*.

1. Samuel and Steven say that Susana is at the library.   True   False
2. The mall is always crowded on Fridays.   True   False
3. Solomon sees Susana at the movie theater.   True   False
4. Solomon is shouting and people are looking at them.   True   False
5. Susana always lies to her parents.   True   False
6. Thomas broke pipes in the building.   True   False
7. Susana was surprised to hear about Bobby and his uncle.   True   False

B Circle the correct answer.

1. Susana is _____ that Bobby is Thomas's nephew.

   a. thankful   **b.** glad   **c.** surprised

2. What do Bobby and Thomas want to do?

   a. They want to work hard.

   b. They want to control Solomon's building.

   c. They want to hire another relative.

3. Solomon surprised Bobby with _____.

   a. a visit from his uncle

   b. a tape recorder

   c. a new apartment

C Write answers to the questions about the story.

1. Describe Solomon's family.

_____

_____

_____

_____

_____

2. Why are Solomon and his family in Miami?

_____

_____

_____

_____

_____

3. What did Mr. Morgan do to Thomas and Bobby?

_____

_____

_____

_____

_____

4. Why do you think Mrs. Clark is on vacation with Solomon and his family?

_____

_____

_____

_____

_____

Work with the Words

A Complete the sentences with the correct words.

bonus	embarrass	lie
crowded	honest	neighborhood

1. He's a very _____ man. He always tells the truth.

2. I love my _____ because it's quiet and the post office and a coffee shop are only two blocks away.

3. I can't find a seat. This bus is very _____.

4. Please don't wear that ugly shirt. You'll _____ me when we go to the restaurant!

5. I sold 20 cars this month, so my boss is giving me a big _____.

6. Sometimes children _____ to their parents when they do something wrong.

B Complete the sentences with the correct words. You don't need every word.

alone	heavy	lonely	tenant
confused	helpful	mad	thankful
disappointed	hold	miss	uncomfortable
fussy	impolite	spend	

1. Solomon wants to _____ time with his family, but he's very busy.

2. Mrs. Clark lives _____.

3. Mrs. Clark likes to call Solomon because she is _____.

4. Mrs. DeVico asks Bobby to _____ her baby for a minute.

5. Mrs. Johnson is very _____ about the repairs in her apartment. The repairs have to be perfect!

6. Belinda was _____ with Thomas because he didn't talk or say "Thank you". But she thought he was _____.

7. Susana was _____ at her father when he fired Bobby.

8. Solomon didn't understand about the problems in the building. He was _____.

9. Mr. Jackson is an elderly _____ in the building.

10. Solomon's family is _____ that they can have a bigger apartment in a new building.

Lifeskill Practice

■ We use these words to talk about work and pay.

Match the words with the pictures.

__c__ **1.** quit   ____ **3.** hire   ____ **5.** lazy

____ **2.** a raise   ____ **4.** a bonus   ____ **6.** fire

a.

b.

c.

d.

e.

f.

Dialogue Practice

Practice the conversation with two classmates.

Susana: Uh, oh! Bobby! My father is here! I'm in big trouble.

Solomon: Susana, what are you doing here with him? You are not with Paulette! Why did you lie to your mother?

Susana: Daddy, be quiet! You're embarrassing me! People are looking.

Solomon: Embarrassing you? Embarrassing you? You lied to your mother. You said that you were going to Paulette's house. I can't believe it! You usually do not lie to us.

Susana: But, Daddy, I . . . I . . .

Solomon: Be quiet, Susana.

Bobby: Mr. Soriano, I'm sorry. I was in your neighborhood, and I saw Susana. I invited her to the movies.

Solomon: Oh, really? That's interesting, Bobby. Today Mr. Morgan hired your uncle, Thomas, to be a new super in my building, and Mr. Morgan says that you are going to come back to work in the building.

Bobby: Oh, you know about Uncle Thomas? Well, this is great. Now we can work together again!

Solomon: Work together? But, Bobby, why do you want to come back to work in my building? You never worked hard before. You were friendly to the tenants, but you didn't help me. The building is old, and now there are many problems in the building. I have to work very hard every day.

Bobby: Problems? Oh, we can fix those problems, Mr. Soriano. Uncle Thomas only broke a few pipes and broke a light or two. He can fix everything in a few hours. He can . . .

Susana: What are you talking about, Bobby?

Bobby: I . . . I mean . . . Uncle Thomas is good at fixing things. He can . . . He can fix all of the . . . problems.

Susana: I don't understand. Daddy, what is Bobby talking about?